CW00541676

Song to the Siren

Song to the Siren

Larry Beckett

Halbaffe Press

Commendations

Some poets teach. Some poets preach. Larry Beckett works. His new collection, Song to the Siren, named for the countlessly covered tune he wrote in collaboration with the late Tim Buckley, is composed of selected lyrics from 1966 to 2023, all exploring the Muse he has courted, sometimes seduced and succumbed to. Close rhymes recall the likes of Walt Whitman, Edgar Lee Masters and Vachel Lindsay, as well as the endlessly calling Greek masters. In the process, he breaks down false distinctions between poetry and song, our longest lasting expression of emotion, which lives outside academic walls. Enter his world, and be inspired.

—Paul Wilner, Contributing Editor,
ZYZZYVA magazine

Larry Beckett is probably best known for writing lyrics, but he has spent his life as a poet, writing epics of American history, adapting old English mythology, composing love poems and almost anything else you could name. This anthology, Song to the Siren, is a collection of his song-based poetry, spanning his work with Tim Buckley, through his later songwriting adventures, to translations of Goethe, right up to his work with Eyelids on their album The Accidental Falls, a record I had the honor of co-producing and playing on. His work is so full of poetic and literary allusions that to properly plumb its depths could take weeks. Or the poems should be read as they appear on the page, simple, heartbreaking and altogether moving. His work has meant much to me through the years. I can only hope that his writing will have the same effect on you.

—Peter Buck, R.E.M.

This luminous collection of lyrics, discerningly selected from song-writer-poet Larry Beckett's vast body of work, is a gift of line to be cherished by music lovers and songwriters alike. A conveyance on waves "steep and holy," emanating from Beckett's "salty heart," these songs of dream and longing, steeped in epic myth, draw ancient archetypes with force and elegance into the present. Not a cheap trick for an artist working within the conventions of popular song, and one Beckett accomplishes with masterful ease. Sharp, yearning, at times mournful, traveling from tenderness to rage, imbued ever with hope, this gathering of lyrics chimes sweetly in modern mode with Boccaccio and Chaucer, bringing its readers into direct and savory encounter with the comedy of life. Song to the Siren—robust, wry, filled with heart, humor, longing, and pathos—far better than answers, voices the questions on which your life just might depend.

—Marc Zegans, poet, author of Lyon
Street and The Underwater Typewriter

Larry Beckett's bardic visions are firmly in the American grain – there's a wide-eyed, big-shouldered vitality to his poetry that suggests Whitman, Sandburg, and Masters, with exotic dashes of Yeats' prophetic scope and Rimbaud's transgressive confessions as well. At the same time, his writings are gritty, funny, and steeped in the homespun vernacular of folk ballads, medicine show spiels, and backroom rock 'n' roll. "Song to the Siren" may be his most celebrated lyric, but its haunting Homeric echoes course through even his evocation of modern-day L.A. and points south. This collection extends from his celebrated days as Tim Buckley's lyricist through the present moment—but whatever era you dip into, Beckett remains the eternally young seeker, encountering an enchanted world that balances delight and sorrow on a finely-honed blade's edge. His writer's touch is classically rooted, yet as immediate in impact as the rising sun. He journeys far and deeply in these pages, and he beckons you to follow. . .

—Barry Alfonso, music journalist

Song to the Siren
© 2024 Larry Beckett

All material in *Song to the Siren* is the property of creator and may not be used or reprinted in any manner without express permission from the author or publisher, except for the quotation of short passages used inside of an article, criticism or review. Printed in the United States of America. All rights reserved. All material in *Song to the Siren* is printed with permission.

First published 2024 by Halbaffe Press.
Halbaffe Press in the US is an imprint of Sinensis Publications, a division of Sinensis LLC, registered in the USA.

ISBN-13:979-8-218-25792-7

First Edition: July 2024

Song to the Siren

The Outcast

All American

My Companion

Old Beauty

Blue Night

Noah's Dove

Music

The Outcast

Los Angeles Riverbed

Climb the pylon high's you dare;
walk over, walk over:
bunch of blackbirds on the crackling wire.
Oh Los Angeles riverbed.

Hide out under the freeway, kid;
walk over, walk over:
with a book of stars and a ship of wood.
Oh Los Angeles riverbed.

Fire your rocket down the riverbed;
walk over, walk over:
look, a jackrabbit in the tumbleweeds.
Oh Los Angeles riverbed.

Fire and fire, and flying in winter
along the concrete river.

Morning-Glory

I lit my purest candle close to my
window, hoping it would catch the eye
of any vagabond who passed it by,
and I waited in my fleeting house.

Before he came I felt him drawing near;
as he neared I felt the ancient fear
that he had come to wound my door and jeer,
and I waited in my fleeting house.

"Tell me stories," I called to the Hobo;
"Stories of cold," I smiled at the Hobo;
"Stories of old," I knelt to the Hobo;
and he stood before my fleeting house.

"No," said the Hobo, "No more tales of time;
don't ask me now to wash away the grime;
I can't come in 'cause it's too high a climb,"
and he walked away from my fleeting house.

"Then you be damned!" I screamed to the Hobo;
"Leave me alone," I wept to the Hobo;
"Turn into stone," I knelt to the Hobo;
and he walked away from my fleeting house.

Rimbaud's Geisha

Is she a geisha? In the blue hour
she'll blow away like a dead flower
in the sea breezes up and down
the boardwalk of the booming town.

It's too gorgeous! But it belongs
to the fishwife, the pirate's songs,
the last dancers in their devotion
to wild nights by the innocent ocean.

Song to the Siren

Long afloat on shipless oceans,
I did all my best to smile
till your singing eyes and fingers
drew me loving to your isle,

and you sang, Sail to me, sail to me,
let me enfold you:
here I am, here I am,
waiting to hold you.

Did I dream you dreamt about me?
Were you hare when I was fox?
Now my foolish boat is leaning
broken, lovelorn, on your rocks,

for you sing, Touch me not, touch me not,
come back tomorrow.
Oh my heart, oh my heart,
shies from the sorrow.

I am puzzled as the oyster,
I am troubled as the tide:
should I stand amid the breakers?
Should I lie with death my bride?

Hear me sing, Swim to me, swim to me,
let me enfold you:
here I am, here I am,
waiting to hold you.

The Outcast of the Islands

(after Joseph Conrad)

1 Captain Lingard

The southern sea's alive
under the stitching sun:
she'll roll you blue with love
and rake you from the bow.

I lean into it still
out where the dolphins down,
running my darling brig
from here to Samarang.

The sea itself is bare
and simple as a hoop,
but her waves are steep and holy
here in my salty heart.

2 Almayer

Sleep on, my eastern daughter,
I'm white as the captain's sails,
and I'm the only trader
under the captain's sky.

I sag on the verandah,
my palm leaf in my fingers,
and slide into the heavens
till the ghosts go away.

3 Babalatchi

I led the Sulu rovers
and now I'm a one-eyed dog,
but the writing on my forehead
is sign my comfort will come.

I'll make my man the rajah
and rig white against white,
till all the pigs on the river
salaam their one-eyed lord.

4 Lakamba

I slump here, fat. Their black
spears on the rail, the faithful
sleep on my bamboo stoop.
Crown me soon, one-eyed man.

They play chess on red clay
and jabber by the thin fires,
but I dream like a bandit
of cobras and the throne.

5 Omar

My sight, my pirate days,
blown both into slivers
by the witch-mothered whites,
I live, all prayers and bones,

my daughter lost, my daughter
loving the white outcast,
the infidels, oh Allah
ram him, stiffen him soon.

6 Aissa

Oh my outcast is a man
strange as the Indian wind,
but I have rooted love
under his solid ribs.

This terror, white as those
who shot my father down,
lies in my lap as I
lean over him like stars.

7 Abdulla

The outcast says he'll steer me
up through the unknown mouth
into the captain's country.
The one-eyed man's an eel.

I'll outshine the captain:
come twilight, I will bow
down to the Holy City,
his river in my fist.

8 The Outcast

I was scared of my abandon
when the cranes were in the east,
but you shimmered by the water
and I became your beast.

The sun on your brown fingers
is like a fisherman's song,
but the sun when you're upriver
is a backbreaking gong.

Oh your eyes are too barbaric,
but the cranes are in the west:
I'm the outcast of the islands,
and my chance is in your breast.

Tijuana Moon

The padre told me all the hymns
were born out of the saxophone,
and I went down to festival
beneath the Tijuana moon.

I saw a fighter and a whore
who broke a love as strong as stone;
I drank myself into a dream
about the Tijuana moon.

Oh you can kick the Texas blues,
tequila and the burning spoon,
but, my amigos, nothing's good
against the Tijuana moon.

My dirty Tijuana moon,
my darling Tijuana moon.

No Man Can Find the War

Photographs of guns and flame,
scarlet skull and distant game,
bayonet and jungle grin,
nightmares dreamed by bleeding men:
lookouts tremble on the shore
but no man can find the war.

Tape recorders echo scream,
orders fly like bullet stream,
drums and cannons laugh aloud,
whistles come from ashen shroud:
leaders damn the world and roar
but no man can find the war.

Is the war across the sea?
Is the war behind the sky?
Have you each and all gone blind:
is the war inside your mind?

Humans weep at human death,
all the talkers lose their breath,
movies paint a chaos tale,
singers see and poets wail:
all the world knows the score
but no man can find the war.

Xmas 2001

They light up all the Christmas boats
across the river, and hymn the child,
but Agamemnon's blood still calls,
in this world's agony, for blood.

The water slides ignorant down
to the Columbia; air strikes killed
more innocents: this carol's cold:
ah Jesus, the new covenant failed.

Wild Roses

It was in another winter
not long after it snowed,
a bus was shifting down
on a blue southern road.

Wild roses, long
in stem and leaf,
and daisies, oh
but they are brief.

Old man at the window
with a heavenly bouquet,
a girl across the aisle
who could not look away.

Wild roses, long
in stem and leaf,
and daisies, oh
but they are brief.

You love the flowers, he said,
and the flow of the sap;
my wife would like for you...
and laid them in her lap.

Wild roses, long
in stem and leaf,
and daisies, oh
but they are brief.

She smiled inside & dreamed
of blossoms when you marry,
watched him get off and walk
into the cemetery.

Wild roses, long
in stem and leaf,
and daisies, oh
but they are brief.

Love Is Strong

He met her in the days of war,
out at the oyster cannery:
they made a house of only drift,
and only love.

He held his peace, like river weeds,
and like the water, she was heard:
sixty years on, he lost his one
and only love.

He laid him down: —I can't stay on.
Get me the suit I's married in.
Oh dear Viola, one last breath,
and only love.

Elegy

Snow is falling
on Plato's grave;
no light is left
in his damn cave;

lilies climbing
through Jesus' bones;
nobody can
roll away stones:

out of pleasure,
out of pain;
I feel like I'm
going to rain.

China, what did
the old man say?
I was immortal
every day.

Babylon

How many miles to Babylon?
Oh they say 3 score and 10.
Can I get there by candlelight?
Yes they say and back again.

I saw a man wrapped in the dark,
hoping nobody'd see his skin;
he asked if I had any change:
41 miles to Babylon.

I saw a woman standing with
a bag of water in the new moon
and her hands tied with an old rope:
21 miles to Babylon.

I saw a kid, oh black and blue,
and writing down a mixed up song
about an airplane that was lost:
1 more mile to Babylon.

By the waters
by the waters of Babylon
there we sat down and wept
when we remembered Zion.

The Rain

Oh crackups on the interstate,
vendetta in the passing lane,
tailgates banging down the line:
blame it on the rain.

I mailed a letter to my girl,
but her reply I can't explain;
it was all too blurred to read:
blame it on the rain.

Been fooled into another war,
can't bear to say they died in vain;
if their ghosts don't care who wins,
blame it on the rain.

I send my songs to Sisyphus;
not looking for things in that vein;
this dream is getting so absurd:
blame it on the rain.

Star Sailor

I am a bee out in the fields of winter,
and though I memorized the slope of water
oblivion carries me on his shoulder:
beyond the suns I speak and circuits shiver,
but though I shout the wisdom of the maps
I am a salmon in the ringshape river.

All American

The Minutes

The morning is a redwing,
it flutters off so soon:
I look out of my window,
and all at once it's noon.

The daylight is a hustler,
the sky is quickly crossed:
I cannot sweep the stairway
before the sun is lost.

And April is so ghostly,
it hits and off it whirls:
the foam on the Missouri
is longer in the world.

The summers pass me over,
the pendulum tells why:
oh there are no more minutes
for Rosalie and I.

Showdown

I've followed you all summer,
but come one spooky day
I'll kill you for the bounty
and ride on flush and high.

The wind is sharp as wine
in the sticks of Carolina:

morning of the showdown,
and the last laugh but one,
you won't have a prayer, boy,
I'm living by the gun.

And when I bag the money,
I wonder what I'll do?
Buy me a blue-eyed hooker
and a pint of foxhead rye.

The weather's looking bad
on the flats of Colorado:

morning of the showdown,
and the last laugh but one,
you won't have a prayer, boy,
I'm living by the gun.

I'm cocking back the hammer,
but I'm cloudy in the eye:
I never saw a green kid
swagger as bright as you.

I hold my powder horn
on the slopes of California:

morning of the showdown,
I fire into the sun;
forgive a loveless drifter
for living by the gun.

Deadwood

Oh Wild Bill, why'd you go down
to the Number Ten saloon?
Old sharpshooter, they dealt you
aces and eights in your last hand.

And so long, Calamity Jane;
hard girl, you were a mama to me.
Guess how they laid you out:
in a white dress, holding two guns.

Oh Deadwood, I'm going home;
you cheated me out of my fun.
Heartbreak hangs in your streets
like the absurd sun over the badlands.

Whiskey all around,
ice man, it's on me:
here's to my old loves
who lie under Mt. Moriah.

Banks of the Ohio

Though all your history's a whirl,
don't do me like a Portsmouth girl
under a moon that's on the wane
and fly around like a weathervane.

You've got the curves, like waves that ride
in veils of white, oh be my bride
and take a vow where the lilacs blow
down by the banks of the Ohio.

Though there's no time in paradise,
we can't step in the same river twice:
the question starts up like a dove,
how can I hold on to my love?

Only say that you'll be mine
and in no other arms entwine
down beside where the waters flow,
down by the banks of the Ohio.

Colorado Trail

Guess I can get some work
up Cheyenne way
if they'll tender this old ghost
any of their pay.

I wasn't made for love,
so hard to know
when to hold her in your arms,
when to let her go.

Don't see the lightning ball,
don't feel the wet;
all I see's her blessed face,
all I feel's regret.

All I have's a ways to go,
dreams that won't fail,
as I cross the mountains on
the Colorado trail.

Mountain Man

Go and bridle my good mule,
I believe I'll hike
out across Salt River ford,
clear up Camelback.

What's a pint of lightning gin
and a twist of pork?
Supper for a mountain man
way up Camelback.

Ragshack Bill, it's adios,
hand me up my sack:
keep my shovel, I ain't digging
gold on Camelback.

When I'm up old Camelback
under blackbird skies,
I'll just light awhile and look
down on paradise.

The All-American Girl

Oh I can sing loud as a mule
and drink till I'm in love.
I've screwed more cowboys than I can count:
I'm the all-American girl.

I ride big broncos, I wrestle longhorns,
I shoot just like a star.
You monkey with me, I'll lay you flat:
I'm the all-American girl.

Showboat

Black face man,
go blow it high,
straight into
the southern sky:

St. Louie's banging
on the ivories,
New Orleans
on slide trombone,

rooty-toot
and razz-ma-tazz,
honky-tonk
and walking jazz,

with a squeal stick
and a rub-a-dub,
with an iron horn
and a tin tub,

with a paddlewheel
and a blowing stack,
with a jolt of jackass
busting my back,

with a hip dancer
down in my arms,
with Dixie glory
and shooting stars,

oh won't you ship me
down old Mississippi,
I want to ride
the showboat!

Corn Cracker

Moon, moon,
shindy in the barn,
I guess I'll take a swallow from
my big Kentucky horn.

Banjo, banjo,
ragging in the pines:
I'm stomping in the hollow till
the stars go rockabye.

Dogfish in a plum tree,
catbird on a pole:
billy goat, nanny goat,
let her roll.

Day, day,
cracking in the east:
nobody but the hoot owl knows
where I am going to roost.

Sweetheart, sweetheart,
sitting on my knee:
we're sailing the Ohio on
a watermelon seed.

Pass Your Light Around

The county jail is solid stone,
the stick of dreams is all you own;
it's Sunday night, you're out of lights,
but if you live you're not alone.

I'll never see my shooting star,
I've been too long on prison farms;
I say a prayer when no one's there
that Marguerite was in my arms.

When Jesse James went on a spree,
he slammed from here to Tennessee;
you can't arrest the wilderness:
down in the hole we still are free.

Pass your light around,
there are no matches,
and by a touch
a fire catches;
light 'em up
and smoke 'em down;
oh won't you please
pass your light around.

Liberty

They can't spy on lightning,
hold rain in captivity,
and do it all for national
security.

Oh my love has iron bones
when the law is just a prayer,
outlasting the Atlantic winds
and looming there:

Liberty,
I see your island, and I see
your starry crown, the waves in chains:
deliver me.

Liberty,
across the harbor, look at me:
you hold the book, you lift the fire
and I am free.

I don't want a border line,
I don't want to history:
what's to come is who I am
and mystery.

Oh my love has copper skin
against the power of the air,
outlasting the Atlantic winds
and looming there:

Liberty,
I see your island, and I see
your starry crown, the waves in chains:
deliver me.

Liberty,
across the harbor, look at me:
you hold the book, you lift the fire
and I am free.

My Companion

Love Lie Down

Your face is like Dixie weather,
your breasts are like lily flowers.
Your daddy's working on the railroad:
oh love lie down, lie down by me.

Your voice is like mountain music,
your legs are like Sunday ponies.
Your mama's sleeping by the cradle:
oh love lie down, lie down by me.

Your belly's like lazy water,
your hips are like books of stories.
A lark is flying round my cabin:
oh love lie down, lie down by me.

Venice

White heat of swaying day:
dark slap of conga cries,
come out and breathe as one;
salt sea and fiddle's drone
out on the dancing stone
while the santanas blow,
and the music boat's in the bay.

Here sunrise was stinging,
full of all our longing.

If you can't give me comfort
at least come for a reel
on the long promenade.

You see old Crazy Ed,
dressed in his sheet of white,
dragging from pier to pier,
hustling his drinking dimes
all for his life of crimes,
until it cracks his heart,
and the music boat's in the bay.

I swear there is summer
sunlight in the water.

If he can get his comfort
he reels wine-blooded down
on the long promenade.

One is for one alone,
two for the tug of war,
three for the shining gods,
four for the love that stands,
five for the hand of man,
six for the rolling bones,
and the music boat's in the bay.

Monterey

Under a loop of stars
in the vulgar cold,
the dead airport lay
by the pebbles of the highway.

Through the snail clouds
you soared to your lover;
I hurried away, my darling,
with a howl in my throat.

Drunk Baby

If you would only lean on me
and look up at the little moon:
all you love's a two-dollar word
and a fifth of that beaujolais.

I'd like to take your crazy talk
and punctuate it with a kiss:
nothing touches your lips but salt,
tequila, and a lemon slice.

Drunk baby, you sure do squawk
when the firewater's in your head:
drunk baby, I'll answer you,
but only in your king-size bed.

The Sun Is Like a Big Brass Band

The sun is like a big brass band
that everyone can hear;
it strikes up by the hot dog stand
and waltzes down the pier.

Oh grab your girl by the hand,
and buy your man a beer:
the sun is like a big brass band
now that my darling's here.

Have a Cigar

Once I was a stargazer,
and she was a free-for-all:
I gave her a rose and a chill;
she gave me a cannonball.

One day while I gave her the works,
I said Let's make it three;
she cried Hold on, you April fool,
you're paradising me!

Now all the rowdydow I know
is in the heart of me:
I'm nothing but her dreamboat,
and she's my jubilee.

Come in your buggy or goose the ghost,
and bring your own dynamite;
with Jersey lightning and a delta band
I'm hitching my bride tonight.

Goethe's Mignon

I wish I was where lemons swing
on flimsy bushes in the back yard,
oranges sun on the green branches
and the air rushes in the palm trees.
If I knew where, I'd fly down there,
down there with you, oh my honey.

I wish I was on the pine porch
of a spare house where the light's lavish,
old movie stars look down and wonder,
Oh baby, what's happened to you?
If I knew where, I'd fly down there,
down there with you, big daddy.

It's way beyond that rainy mountain
where pickup trucks turn into mist,
wildcats screw in the alcove cut
by the spray of the accidental falls.
If you know where, don't fool around here:
oh muscle man, let's get rolling.

Across the Persian Gulf

Oh I wish you were a slave girl
on fire like all the eastern stars,
and sailing free on my crescent sloop
across the Persian Gulf:

but you go dancing in the Rosebud Bar
and look for love in the awkward dark,
and mornings I load cargo at the docks
on ships that melt away.

Love Is on the Street

Loosen up with me;
oh your eye is cold:
love is on the street,
and the moon is old.

This morning I was a lazybones,
but tonight I'm a drifter:
love is on the street,
and the moon is old.

Across the Highway

You're in the weeds across the highway,
and the stars buzz around the moon;
and the traffic booms between us,
but I can hear you crying on.

It's too easy to love the sailor
and the dirty dancer in the blue bar;
and there's no sting, oh there's no riddle
in my old kiss and this raw year.

I can't console you like your sisters
and I can't sell you talking tough,
but I'll shove over the loud highway:
I'm still with you, my only wife.

I Love a Waitress

I love a waitress,
she's working late:
she says she loves me,
I wait and wait.
I guess I'm easy,
I won't pretend:
she's like the daylight
at winter's end.

It's only me, joking around with Don Quixote,
while Lord Jim's opening up a six-pack of beer;
Odysseus wants to watch an old movie tonight,
and David Copperfield's looking for a storybook;
Huck Finn's hoping to learn to play ragtime piano,
and Robinson Crusoe's boning up on his algebra;
Hamlet's at the desk, grinding out a good sonnet,
and Sherlock Holmes is here untangling it all.
Oh I could dance like a dolphin but it's no fun
now she doesn't come home when her shift is done.

I love a waitress,
she's working late;
she says she loves me,
I wait and wait.
I guess I'm easy,
I won't pretend:
she's like the daylight
at winter's end.

Don't You Leave Cheyenne

Don't you leave Cheyenne,
it's the promised land.

It's the last dance now
that you broke your vow.

Don't you leave Cheyenne
if you give a damn.

Oh you stars above,
yes, I'm still in love.

Don't you leave Cheyenne
with a Denver man.

My Blue Piano

It was freezing, remember,
the January night
when I kissed you two times,
oh, and you kissed me one.

Oh the boats rock around,
and the stars roll away.
Where do marriages go
in a couple of years?

There's a jet to California,
and Apollo to the moon,
but they can't fly me back
to the early days.

If I can't be your husband,
if I can't, oh my love,
can I play just a little
on my blue piano?

One-Minute Love Affair

I adored a girl I saw by chance
walking Broadway this morning:
I held her hard in my blue eyes
in my one-minute love affair.

When I go over the salty years
we were man and wife,
oh my daydreamer, it's like it was
just a one-minute love affair.

Oh shapely as a banjo tune
and sharp as a star in July,
with a face like roses in the bud
was my one-minute love affair!

Sugar Daddy

You can kiss your sailor,
it's okay by me:
I'm just scared he'll drift from you
and stick you with your love.

Sailors flirt and in a flash
oh, they haul away:
in your sugar daddy's arms
you'll forget the sea.

If you lose your sweetheart,
come to my feather bed:
I don't ask your faithful love,
just screw me like you care.

Wear my pearls
for your man tonight;
but morning, who'll comfort you?
Oh, your sugar daddy.

Song to the Air

Pop music's coming through the wall,
cats bang in the back yard;
there's nothing on tv tonight,
I sing but it's absurd;
I look up from my piano at
old glory: every star
was stolen from the indians
for my song to the air.

My daddy plays the horses
and my mama walks the greens;
my sister raises kids like her,
my brother pigs and beans:
they never read a canto
of the comedy of fire,
and so what if they never ask
for my song to the air?

I know this blonde, who'll whip me out
self-portraits for a price;
her lover aims his camera
but never at my face:
I go to see them at their shows,
they shoot by in a blur
with no idea if I'm still working
on my song to the air.

The man next door sells life insurance,
his customers are fat;
his woman wears a uniform,
his kid is in for it;

he says things like nuclear defense,
he's fixing for a war:
but I can't change an atom
with my song to the air.

My partner, at his harmonium,
is counting on a hit;
I caroled to his ex-wife, while
she lectured me on art:
if New York is an egghead
then Hollywood's a whore;
this rainy town is nothing much
to my song to the air.

Oh my companion's first in beauty,
that's why she cheats on me;
she listens to my mysteries
and then she steals away:
she arm-in-armed with me to Florence,
I'm grateful for that hour;
it's her complexities I sing
in my song to the air.

Today I walked with Dante's ghost,
I saw his skinny face;
I was charged up by his vulgar tongue,
his love for Beatrice:
like him, I live in exile,
though I was born right here,
and scrawl like all I'll ever be
is my song to the air.

Italian Journey

Oh I was only twenty,
on the waterfront, unknown:
and she was like a slant of wind
into all quarters blown.
The morning I saw Florence
and the bridge where Dante sighed
bows to the one I first was eye-
to-eye with Manda Bradlyn.

And on the winter solstice
her bridesmaid was the moon:
we married, oh but grounded on
the day-to-day too soon.
That afternoon in Venice
beside the green canal
brought back my vow to always arm-
in-arm with Manda Bradlyn.

Oh I'm no fortune teller
or fortune teller's son:
I may bang on from girl to girl
or anchor at last with one.
But tonight above Ravenna
in the mosaic of fire
I read the stars that say I'll be
in love with Manda Bradlyn.

Second Avenue

In the hissing street, that old girl goes
with a newspaper over her bowed head,
and I blow my hands and walk on hard
in the fool's rain on Second Avenue,

all the holes closed for the night
and the bad wine wearing off,
and nothing for the cold but that fire
in an iron barrel, my knowledge of you.

Old Beauty

All I Can Do Is Dance

Oh California, your sky is bare,
the stars are in your streets;
and I'm so blue I'd write a book
but all I can do is dance.

Oh money keeps me up all night,
and love puts me to bed;
the sun comes up like my favorite song,
and all I can do is dance.

Starlight

I owe my voice to a fiction,
and my nickname to a fan;
I owe my voice to a fiction,
and my face to the make-up man.

I am the whip of the season,
till I return my routine;
I am the whip of the season,
I am a limelight machine.

Mama, raise the rag,
I'm going on;
daddy, hit the lights,
I'm going on.

Diddledeedum, diddledeedum,
huftymagufty, my queen;
diddledeedum, diddledeedum,
I am a limelight machine.

Old Beauty

I signed on with a western show,
I loved the manager's daughter:
they promised me a dollar a song
if I'd give up old beauty.

One morning I was fired for nothing,
my girl shoved on without me:
oh now I'd sing and all for free
just to get back old beauty.

On the Hook

I saw the gypsy woman
and drank her rum and coke;
You'll never be a dream, she said,
till you go up in smoke.

I saw the country doctor
and I showed him my star;
You're sick of rock-and-roll, he said,
haul out your old guitar.

I'm walking on the clouds,
I'm on the hook all right;
I'll kick you in the morning,
oh love me up tonight.

Elvis Presley

It was dark, oh you Memphis cock,
till with feathers on fire
you crowed to the red sexual sun
all of your country blues.

Oh death can't bust my radio,
you loud Las Vegas showboat:
sing natural opera, and rock me
with one more country blues.

John Lennon

We listen to old rock-and-roll
under the comeback sun,
my girl and I, and talk of kids,
but oh, where's John?

I watched the game that winter night
the newsman said he's gone:
imagine there's no heaven, oh
then oh, where's John?

I sent my love to Yoko, and
dear Julian and Sean,
but all that they could answer me
was oh, where's John?

I don't know why that man cracked up
or who sold him the gun:
it's you and I who make the laws,
and oh, where's John?

That little war, the English let
the Argentine boys down
into the waves, and who spoke out,
and oh, where's John?

I love the earth, like always, but
it's hard to write a song:
it's not as good as it once was,
and oh, where's John?

Jeff Buckley

The papers said
the American Queen
saw you, washing
up, at Beale Street:

who else, after
the King, could hold
the microphone
and so sing live?

Only, after
ah the last, dream
brother, go back
to grace, the first.

After the Last

I saw your daddy ache in his skin
none could redeem.
What was his fury? Only the grace
to be a dream.

Newspaper said the American Queen
down at Beale Street
saw you wash up: father of waters,
song incomplete.

After the last,
dream brother,
sing me the first,
dream brother.

After the King, who else could hold
that microphone
and do it live? Children, take care
of flesh and bone.

All of the years, under the moon,
go down the stream:
music is fire, and I can hear
only in dream.

After the last,
dream brother,
sing me the first,
dream brother.

Synchronicity

In winter, electricity,
lyrics from cyberspace,
Wild Roses, sent to me
for music, out of grace.

Synchronicity:
what light, like divinity,
is carried by invisible
rivers uniting you and me.

In her diary, my first
solo with that brass band;
and oh, I read the name:
Wild Rose, in her lost hand.

Synchronicity:
what light, like divinity,
is carried by invisible
rivers uniting you and me.

Blue Night

Origin

The dark, a man,
a woman, light;
at last they met;
he loved at sight:

she lit out, left
him memories,
and you and I
are made of these.

We Want a Touchdown

Go! Go!
Where? Where?
We want a touchdown
over there!

She'd cartwheel when the boys were up
and flash her ass hooray,
and she always sang when it was tough
for Abraham Lincoln High.

She was honey, she was mama,
and now she's years ago:
we parked one night on palm tree street,
she was lolling across from me!

We shot the bull till the sun came out
and all the time we talked
about Moby Dick and Fats Domino
we were dying for a fuck.

I never rock-and-rolled her, oh
I never touched her tits;
I never balled my pom-pom girl,
I only kissed her good night.

Go, go:
where, where:
we want a touchdown
over there.

Found at the Scene of a Rendezvous that Failed

Kill the candle, close the door, and take a bow:
there's only lunacy now.
Drink the lemon, eat your words, and swallow time:
remember my touch is a crime.

Catch the cancer-frozen leaves without your net:
paint me in black silhouette.
Burn the flying fish of memory tonight:
flutter and fall like a kite.

For there's nowhere to go,
no windows but walls:
last night I broke a key;
you're good as dead to me:
oblivion calls

Damn the stars and wait five seasons, I will come,
playing hello on my drum.
Drive the vagabonds away, deny the thieves:
hide all your smiles up your sleeves.

Keep the flower in your palm and fall asleep:
wake up in drunkenness deep.
Laugh at lawyers, trick the judge, and ditch the trial:
one day I'll land on your isle.

Still there's nowhere to go,
no wonders begun:
this morning I was cold;
today we're ruled and told:
tomorrow we'll run.

Apollinaire's Gypsy

The gypsy knew it in advance
Our lives divided by the nights
We said goodbye to her and then
Out of that hole Hope's lights

Dancing on two feet as we liked
Love was as heavy as a bear
And the bluebird lost its plumes
The panhandler his prayer

We're no angels but in the hopes
Of love and on the road we hold
Hands as we go thinking of all
The gypsy had foretold

Dance for Me, Anna Lee

The sky is always cloudy
and yet it just can't rain,
but I can see the lightning
and hear the hurricane.

I loved a girl from Phoenix;
her wings were weak and bare,
and when she got her feathers
she faded in the air.

And here's another dollar,
and turn the song so high,
and I will watch you dancing
while love goes sailing by.

The Brooklyn Girl

When I was on the road,
oh mama, I betrayed
the Brooklyn girl.
If you like a lowdown song,
I'll play:
oh my banjo's blue today.

There's no lady can hold her own
like the Brooklyn girl:
love is the loyalty
she always showed to me.

Old mountains, all in ice,
I'll pine until I kiss
the Brooklyn girl.
If you like a lowdown song,
I'll play:
it goes, Brooklyn's far away.

Marlene's Lullaby

It's twelve but it's the blowhard horns,
no New Year's kiss for me.
Oh sleep tight baby, I'm all worn out
and morning is on the way.

Your daddy is a two-hearted man,
he's juiced and won't be home.
Oh kid I promise I'll be your cradle
and rock you till it's okay.

The Whiskey Moon

If you go back without a word
and no lover on your arm,
oh I'll be nothing but a swallow
above a Sweet Home farm.

Oh the day will be breaking soon,
and you'll miss the whiskey moon.

If I go back without a kiss,
with a shiver of liberty,
oh you'll be nothing but a song
to this poor melody.

Oh my heart will be breaking soon,
if I miss the whiskey moon.

I like to drift into a book,
you like to walk in the weather:
oh why can't we trade worlds beneath
the whiskey moon together?

Oh the day will be breaking soon;
I can see the whiskey moon.

The Rose

Oh honey, your heart's like the jazz
boiling at the last call:
you swallow your one-dollar whiskey,
and offer me a rose.

Don't you flirt with a blue moon boy
after the moon is down:
oh don't you dare look so lovely,
it hurts to hold a rose.

Yeah, head back to your history,
dream down in his old arms:
and this rough morning, forgive me
if I let go the rose.

Blue Night

Lie back; I love the white
pearls around your throat,
the way your hands flutter
over your head like doves.
Sweat beads up on your tits
like rain on the lilies outside,
and your cunt's holding on
like a monkey to a pole.

This mattress is our island
and the radio's our god;
you shiver like a pony
that only I can ride.
I touch you on the spine,
freeze like you're on a rein;
I slap you on the hip,
buck under me like water.

I circled you all evening
in that so hot cage;
now you'll jump through
a hoop on fire for me.
Oh claw me like a lion
as I lace into you;
I'll turn you into music
with my ever-loving cock.

Oh girl,
the blue night's almost gone:
I'll fuck you
till the stars go down.

Bad Girl

She shakes her tangles as she says
she's sorry, she was wrong;
she smiles so shy and pouts her lips:
bad girl wants to blow me.

She strips down to her midnight lace
and slips down to her knees:
she loves that cock like number one,
and kisses it to show me.

She licks me like a sugar cane,
she moans oh and I'm in;
she holds her hair so I can see
her rocking like a boat.

I was bitter a minute back
but she sucks me to the limit:
Jesus, I can't help but shoot
forgiveness down her throat.

Love's Outlaws

First light, your unguarded eye,
salt water, your frail shoulders,
white sandbank, your little breasts,
all innocence or none,
you're out to walk the boardwalk and
go hear that reggae music,
kiss, haul off our rags, and fuck
through the long afternoon.

Billy the Kid with a yellow rose
for his Mexican lady,
love's outlaws are on the loose
all day Saturday:
oh graceful as a southern cloud
and awkward as a pony,
it's revolution in the sun
but I'm the man for you.

The cuckoo sees it's almost twelve
and whistles, Is it illusion?
I'm in your circle like a ship
out on the leaning sea.
Hard cock, bare cunt: I sing this hymn
because we're in blue heaven;
baby, don't go till you see
that first star, way up high

Dreamboat

I recollect a poker hand
like bourbon over ice;
you rode me home in your mama's car
that night of mysteries.
White stars were falling in the air,
the harbor under snow;
and there she lay, her anchor down,
the dreamboat.

I sang ballads in books of matches
all eighty-one alone
till like the new year you hauled in
salvation from the east.
Oh and too soon the sky was red,
I heard a whistle blow:
she was steaming out into the dark,
the dreamboat.

The days stack up like sailor's mail,
the weather's fair for now;
I walk down to the waterfront,
a barge is sliding by.
I hang on to an image in
the absurd foam below:
roll back before it all dissolves,
oh dreamboat.

Venice

I see the city you loved in motion
and lost to circumstance like me one year,
its sun-faded palazzos, its arches and iron,
oh Venice, this evening, isn't so far.

The gondolas rocking on the grand canal,
the islands, the lilacs, the lovers, the squares:
it's too romantic but here by the river,
in your green eyes, Venice isn't so far.

In color, on paper, you mirror its image;
you're like this water, now sliding, now sure:
I can't describe you, I only can love you,
and signal that Venice isn't so far.

Oh that July moon is rising and setting,
but I'm like the stars, I'll always be there,
my arm coming under and my cock inside you
till you sigh Venice isn't so far.

I believe in nothing but your sea-going kisses,
you have an old steady and vacillate on the shore:
is that the basilica, or only a cloud?
Is it true Venice isn't so far?

If you hang back with him, if he is your angel,
I'll hope you're in heaven wherever you are:
I'll finger my blue piano and remember
that evening when Venice wasn't so far.

If you shove off with me we'll be all night making
a girl like the water or a boy like the stars,
and when the sun's up out our eastern window,
it's Venice, oh sweetheart, it isn't so far.

Bad Faith

I was burning up in the white chevy,
no gift, and going away:
It's not that I don't care, was all
the moon moved you to say.
Nine kisses, and like smoke backsliding
to the hard astronomer,
you wrote, Aren't women horrible?
oh angel, in bad faith.

I was fire-walking, and for what?
no sex, no souvenirs
but the dead iris out in the trash,
now that the moon is down.
Go jellyfish from man to man,
oh ex, fuck who you like:
don't say I was your up-and-coming,
I was only insurance.

The Holy Sacramento

Oh the time by
the holy Sacramento,
lilies and cattails
waving by a girl.

She saw love in
the slow delta water,
man and wife working
on a dream house.

He comes home from
his vodka romances:
oh the high weeds,
and the horses loose.

Winter Blues

Oh the blues are blowing
from the east on me,
like a Colorado blizzard
easy to foresee.
Blackbird on the wire,
blackbird in the yard,
whistle once and tell me
why I fall so hard.

The weeds are frozen,
everything's unknown:
I know you're off limits
and walk on alone.
Oh it's in the gospel,
seek and you shall find:
snow is on the river,
you are on my mind.

Come on, baby, out
in the zero-degree:
when I see you, there's
fire inside of me.
I can take the winter,
I can take the wind:
say you will meet me
at the other end.

True Words

Last winter, in that poor
and salty town,
I found the lost hotel
by accident.
Wild rain all night, and in
the morning, oh
I saw you in the heat
of Mexico.

Your face was blazing, like
the light that burns
on the dark waves
of the sea of Cortez.
And the blue day I drove
back to the States,
I kept on hearing you
repeat my name.

Now the snow's piling
on the black pines,
and your religion is
a thousand miles.
All my true words won't say
it in your tongue,
oh my desire, and so
I have to sing.

Boston

How does that city spin
her iron spells:
in our old times, or in
the loyal bells?

Is she a woman or
another station?
This train is looking for
my destination.

Dante's Answer

Love's been my rider, as I go round
the sun, since I was nine:
she bridles and jabs me; under her
I joy, whinny with pain.

I talk logic or values with her,
but I might as well neigh
to the hammering rain, and make
believe it'll end the free-

for-all up in the booming clouds.
I know, in the far turn
of this horse race, that I'm not free:
advice is in vain

now in my flanks I feel new spurs,
and my old nag is slower,
oh and the first filly who leads
me on, I hightail after.

Mermaid Blues

I saw her swimming with
mirror in hand
and in her light I lost
the sight of land,
but I will never lose
the mermaid blues.

I saw her comb her hair,
I was absurd;
call it illusion, but
her song's the word:
it's nothing I can choose,
the mermaid blues.

I saw her breasts were bare;
was that for me?
They warned me going leagues
beneath the sea
to liquid rendezvous:
the mermaid blues.

This coil of memories
may drag me down,
and chasing her tail I
can't help but drown,
with my bones in the ooze:
the mermaid blues.

Thorn & Rose

I heard you play the song of songs
once, on your disillusioned lute,
out of the windows of the moon
I had to shoot.

Why was I ever born,
I ask the thorn.
Heaven only knows,
answers the rose.

I rode Apollo and in vain:
not you, only the desolate shore;
I wavered like the light of earth
and the old war.

Why are the waters torn,
I ask the thorn.
Because the white moon glows,
answers the rose.

Though the moon is in memory,
the smoke of kisses is returning
oh, to the alphabet of fire,
and I am burning.

Why am I made to mourn,
I ask the thorn.
We love what comes and goes,
answers the rose.

River

Oh listen and you'll pick up what
I hiss in syllables of water;
all I wear is bubbles of air:
I'm at the bottom of the river.

Kiss me I slap, slap me I kiss,
I've had enough of love me tender,
old nights, with the double-crosser:
I'm at the bottom of the river.

Love or freedom, I had to choose
the half moon said, and I forgive her;
I got the ghost or woman blues:
I'm at the bottom of the river.

The lovers sway under the sails
and look into the stars and shiver;
the boat slips on, its wake is gone:
I'm at the bottom of the river.

Love & Trial

1 Flux

Flux is a motorcycle blowing down
straight avenue, and the mean street:
when it's burning or dragging, we
are blessed or beat.

Out there, unrest, and rage and hurt,
strong love, old friends in grace;
I remember what all's gone down:
it left a trace.

She and he, young, and tangled in
true love, a world without end ring:
you, if you live by passion, listen
to what I sing.

Though it's a parable, it might
inspire you to a kiss, one night.
and sure, if love, then trial, but
it turns out right.

2 Exile and the Kingdom

She is the window, in the weather,
and he the vigil, down below,
in heart to heart, the fugitive hour,
and time to go.

The west is thunder, the east is red,
but they see only eye to eye:

the old hotel is rocking like
the last goodbye.

Who has the language for the sun
the morning of that fare-thee-well?
Ah grace, who has the breath to give,
the tongue to tell?

This world's my island
of exile, oh
but it's the only
kingdom I know.

3 Wild Rose

She asks him, Love, are you a dream,
ghost of a crash, in my blue eyes,
hallucination, or you, at last
out of disguise?

He answers, I am your long lost;
she lets go tears, but they are few,
not like the fires of other years,
like morning dew.

Oh the wild rose, in all its blush,
may sag in snow, and lose its grace:
in sun, it blooms for love, as in
her living face.

Insomnia

No stars falling
on this ghost town:
ashes, ashes,
nobody's down.

No water falling
off of Hawk Hill:
Jack is up there
waiting for Jill.

She's my insomnia,
lie down in vain.
Nothing ever falls:
only the rain.

Dream

In her eyes the salt
of the seven seas,
in her eyes salvation:
underneath her silk
is the Milky Way,
and her constellation.

If she is there
in where or when,
oh let me dream
again.

On her lips the song
of the morning stars,
on her lips the honey:
heaven up above,
fire down below,
and the two are one.

I said my prayers,
I said amen:
oh let me dream
again.

The light
dims away:
the night
is my day.

In her eyes the salt
of the seven seas,
in her eyes salvation:
underneath her silk
is the Milky Way,
and her constellation.

If she is there
in where or when,
oh let me dream
again.

At Sea

She is the breaking wave,
she is the way to paradise,
and the danger in the blue
oh of the ocean of her eyes

Out in the rain downtown
is where I take my liberty
but I feel her memory kiss,
oh mercy, and I'm lost at sea.

Noah's Dove

Noah's Dove

It's morning, but that quarter moon's
in your grey heaven still;
at the sagging docks the jobs all flash
like pigeons out of my hands.
I ask a down-and-out sailor
for an illegal load,
but he'll call the sheriff if I say that
you are Noah's dove, Laura.

I dreamed I kissed you between the breasts,
I woke up to the rain
with the boat listing on the bad water
of the white Columbia.
If there's a chance I'm going down
I'll radio the shore,
but they won't acknowledge if I say that
you are Noah's dove, Laura.

The marina's thick with masts tonight
as we walk down Union Street
now that your lover's gone to Texas
for a week or more.
I made a song out of superstition
and waltzes in the air:
I'll be saying as you fly away
oh you are Noah's dove, Laura.

Outlaw Moon

She's airy, and just twenty-one,
with grey indifferent eyes;
she blows so cold, but how I wish
she'd steal away with me.
The moon was floating in a light
abstracted from the sun:
by morning it was like a dove
that dazzles and is gone.

We danced so tight to the blues band,
but she had her Texas love,
and now oh God, I ask the wall,
will I get one more chance?
On a slow train through the Siskiyous
I saw the outlaw moon:
no matter how high up we rolled
it was just as remote.

Talking Gypsy

Oh the talking gypsy stood six years
and sang to the white building,
and the hard walls and the woman heard
the love in his throat rising.
That day she kicked off her high heels
made of Spanish leather:
she pulled on her flat heel shoes
and walked out to the highway.

Her old man home, he asked where she
was off to late and early;
his neighbor told him in six words:
she's gone with the talking gypsy.
He slipped into his dirty Ford
and gassed it for the journey:
he swore to drive all day and night
and catch up with his baby.

Oh he turned east and then out west
in that uncertain April:
he thought back and he let go tears
because he was in trouble.
How can you leave Phoenix, he said,
the sun, and all the money?
How can you goodbye your old man
and go with the talking gypsy?

The dove is in his songs, she said,
the rainbow's on his shoulders:
I wouldn't give his kiss for all
your real estate and silence.

Last night I slept in the bright southwest
on your cold loving terms:
tonight I'll sleep out of the rain
in the talking gypsy's arms.

The Twenty-Sixth of June

I banged it over, but the old
green pitcher didn't break;
the sullen radio was playing
Under a blue moon:
the flux of spring was lost on me,
dear music froze inside;
oh but it came rolling out
the twenty-sixth of June.

The letter from Salt River said,
I miss the wind and rain;
I opened up my warped door, like
I'd landed on the moon:
one night, under the crazy quilt,
one week by the true bay,
and all's a shower of love, ah! since
the twenty-sixth of June.

Ceremony

No vows—but who can keep a vow?
I said my line, My love for you
isn't written in the heavens,
and yet it's to
this act all of my days have led.
She said, I'm surrounded by what
I love, the old-time firs, the rain—
and then she cut

off, laughing? no; I saw her tear,
her heart. In a moment, my hand
on her bare shoulder, she went on:
rain shimmering, and
your open arms. A whirl, a wedding,
and oh from that green night to this
I haven't crossed the bridge of dreams
without her kiss.

Passion

Ask why was I so ripe to marry:
not stars or custom,
not looks, hard promises, or money,
not faith. Passion.

Ask why will I conceive a daughter:
not hope or insurance,
not books or pressure, not as a mirror,
not thought. Passion.

Lullaby

Though you float in a heaven dark
outside of the haze of dreams,
I can see daddy's candles, sun, moon,
streetlights and galaxies.

Don't be anxious: you'll inherit all
that dazzles, oh baby, so
rockabye, I'll surround you till
the morning we're eye to eye.

Oh Susannah

Who came out of the book of songs?
And who made up the moon?
Who is walking like a dancer?
I wonder, oh Susannah.

Old banjo, who is the true love
I saw up the dream hill?
Who is shining like the answer?
I wonder. Oh Susannah.

Liam's Eyes

Oh I compute all blessed day,
numbers are only lies,
newspapers blow, and I walk home
to Liam's eyes.

He sang the morning he was born,
and what a fine sunrise:
is that my boyhood in the blue
of Liam's eyes?

I'll never lift a hand to him,
and so the old hand dies:
oh all I care is do I shine
in Liam's eyes.

I'll walk by him far as I can
under the dreaming skies
that bless us with the light to look
in Liam's eyes.

To Leda

You opened for the god,
in shape of swan,
the day after the flood,
the night the man

I was sang you the dove,
and so you bore,
out of the one egg, love,
the other, war,

but what's miracle done
to our old line:
our daughter, oh our son,
mortal, divine.

Paradise

They say that paradise is far
and in another sphere,
but I have looked into your eyes
and I know that it's here.

And when the stars are fading like
the music of the rains,
I will hold you skin to skin
till only love remains.

And when I'm on the other shore,
beyond the veil of blue,
I'll turn my back on the angels
and look homeward to you.

They say that when the flood was all
over the holy land,
Noah's dove came fluttering
and it lit on his hand.

To Kieran

I leave you, in
this testament
of dreams, all that
dazzles, the scent

of star jasmine
in summer air,
the ragged night,
lightning, and prayer,

laughing at nothing,
the Milky Way,
the muscular sun,
another day,

prelude and fugue,
a wave, that scroll,
the double helix,
the quantum soul,

girls, their glances,
and backward boys,
first kiss, the way
of rain, and poise,

the angel by you
on down the line
till you grandfather
and lift the wine,

The Tempest, after
the flood, the dove:
I leave you, as
I leave you, love.

Music

1, 2, 3

1, 2, 3
and the ghost goes home:
ashes, ashes
that the waters comb.

4, 5, 6
and the fight is on:
old love, new love
till the cold is gone.

7, 8, 9
and the fireworks blow:
magic, magic
in the stars below.

10, 11, 12
though the waters rock,
we remember
and the ghost will walk.

Winter, spring
is what we have to sing,
summer, fall
on this sea-breaking ball.

What Was It

What was it that I said,
or I forgot to say?
No answer in the bells,
and from the past, no words.

Oh where is anyone,
inside the foolproof houses?
No answer in the alley,
and from the fire, no words.

When did I lose my touch,
I just can't do without?
No answer in the dark,
and from deep six, no words.

Why is the night so long
and longing so absurd?
No answer in the wine,
and from the moon, no words.

I put a question to the air
as ten years rise and set:
oh who on earth will talk to me
in the soft alphabet?

If It's Magic

If it's magic,
what if it's black, and yet I kissed her:
I am falling
like snow into the river.

Oh cold morning,
all I've done is try and write a letter:
it's paralyzing,
foul up a line and lose her.

I'm skin and bones
but I don't think of that
in the perfect chair
in the revolving room.

If it's love, oh
it's not paradise, when her advances
are uncertain
and she's my only fire.

In the Back

In the back room
I saw the new
moon in his dark
arms and shivered.

Oh we were two
in love with her
crescent till his
voice and fury

warped into waves:
seven years I
listened to birds,
no other song.

Oh the Story

Oh the story goes,
she, without a father,
was conjured up
out of nine blossoms:

wild strawberry, broom,
starflower, rose,
white clover, foxglove,
apple, nettle, oak.

Though all this charm
is only illusion,
one look at her
and I am in love.

In a poet's clothes,
I am here to court her
in all the roads
under the Milky Way:

and when the music starts
she invites me,
her fingers white
as the ninth wave.

How Do I

How do I sing
love and magic
around the moon
oh all night long,

with a tongue of
light outshining
rivals, riddle
me; my old, my

only answer:
whatever she
says I can hear
when the wind blows.

Love in Return

Love in return,
all we ask at
the wishing well:
oh! to arm-in-arm.

We have to wait
and see, day in,
day out: at last
the moon is full.

Like a red mare out in the hills,
she can't be caught
with a lasso all summer, but
I talk her in.

Now and a year from now,
oh! we'll dance around:
this time, I'll count the stars
and she'll return in love.

I Don't Know

I don't know how,
but the winter rains
have turned into
the dear wild roses:

it's a long story
and a short song,
like how my true
love came to me.

Like the sea air,
that woman moved in;
I chased her north,
just out of the army.

In a few years,
the marriage was broke;
I met the next
on a grand tour.

Oh we did flirt,
but discovery was friction;
it's up in smoke,
and oh my! her sister.

I Have Loved

I have loved
oh Shenandoah's daughter:
I lost her, I lost her;
memory is water.

I have touched
the fair and tender ladies:
and I left them looking
at the morning stars.

I have vowed,
dance with the buffalo gal:
we wrangle, we tangle
under the old moon.

I have sung,
oh she is Noah's dove:
our ring's on her finger,
baby in her arms.

I'd explain
but I just want to catch
up with that
white goddess on the road.

The Song

The woman I love
is long and tall;
she moves her body. . .
Only the song.

Ah siren, sing:
she's lost, by choice,
and I am north.
Only the song.

How my heart beat.
She's ghost, and I
will follow her.
Only the song.

When the century
is dust, what will
be left of us?
Only the song.

1966 — 2023
Venice, California
Portland, Oregon

Notes

The Outcast

Los Angeles Riverbed. 1973. Music: Jerry Yester. Recording: Lovin'
Spoonful Spring Demo; Yester. Larry Beckett: private.

Morning-Glory. 1967. Music: Tim Buckley. Recording: Goodbye
and Hello.

Rimbaud's Geisha. 1982. Translation of Est-elle almée,
Arthur Rimbaud.

Song to the Siren. 1967. Allusions to *The Odyssey*, Book XII,
Homer. Music: Tim Buckley. Recording: Tim Buckley,
Starsailor; Morning Glory; This Mortal Coil; single, It'll End
in Tears; Nicola Walker Smith, Black Flowers; Robert Plant,
Dreamland; Damon & Naomi, Song to the Siren: Live in San
Sebastian; Diana Rosalind Land, Same Same—But Different;
John Frusciante, The Empyrean; Sinead O'Connor, Music of
Ireland; Bryan Ferry, Olympia; George Michael, White Light;
Alfie Boe , Alfie Live; Dead Can Dance, In Concert; Jann Klose,
Mosaic; Stuart Anthony and the Long Lost Band, single; Kitty
Macfarlane, Tide & Time; many others.

The Outcast of the Islands. 1973. Song cycle. Based on the novel *An
Outcast of the Islands*, Joseph Conrad.

Tijuana Moon. 1973. Music: Tim Buckley. Recording: Look at the
Fool. Music: Jerry Yester. Recording: Yester.

No Man Can Find the War. 1967. Music: Tim Buckley. Recording:
Goodbye and Hello.

Xmas 2001. 2001.

Wild Roses. 2014. Music: Stuart Anthony. Recording: One More
Mile.

Love Is Strong. 2004. Music: Larry Beckett. Recording: private.

Elegy. 2008.

Babylon. 1992. Quotations from nursery rhyme, Psalm 137. Music:
Jerry Yester. Recording: Lovin' Spoonful Spring Demo; Larry
Beckett: private. Music: 2015, Stuart Anthony: One More Mile.

The Rain. 2007. Music: Larry Beckett. Recording: private.

Star Sailor. 1970. Music: Tim Buckley. Recording: Starsailor.

All American

The Minutes. 1971. Music: Jerry Yester. Recording: Pass Your Light
    Around. Music: 2018, Chris Slusarenko. Recording: Eyelids,
    The Accidental Falls.
Showdown. 1971. Music: Jerry Yester. Recording: Phoenix 9.
Deadwood. 1977. Music: Jerry Yester. Recording: private.
Banks of the Ohio. 1999. Music: Banks of the Ohio, American song.
    Recording: private.
Colorado Trail. 1995. Music: Colorado Trail, American song.
    Recording: private.
Mountain Man. 1971. Music: Jerry Yester. Recording: private.
The All-American Girl. 1975. Music: Larry Beckett. Recording:
    private.
Showboat. 1972. Music: Jerry Yester. Recording: Jerry Yester, Pass
    Your Light Around.
Corn Cracker. 1971. Music: Jerry Yester: Recording: Jerry Yester,
    Pass Your Light Around; Larry Beckett, private.
Pass Your Light Around. 1969. Music: Larry Beckett. Recording:
    Jerry Yester, Pass Your Light Around.
Liberty. 2013

My Companion. For Manda Bradlyn Beckett.

Love Lie Down. 1975. Music: Polegnala e Todora, Bulgarian song,
    arranged by Jerry Yester. Recording: Larry Beckett, private;
    Catherine Guard, private; Jerry Yester, Just Like the Big Time.
    Publication: *Songs and Sonnets*.
Venice. 1969. Music: Tim Buckley. Recording: Boboquivari, tv show.
Monterey. 1970. Music: Tim Buckley. Recording: Starsailor. Music:
    2018, Chris Slusarenko. Recording: Eyelids, The Accidental Falls.
Drunk Baby. 1979. Music: Larry Beckett. Recording: private. Music:
    Jerry Yester. Recording: Phoenix 9.
The Sun Is Like a Big Brass Band. 1974. Music: Aus meines herzens
    grunde, J. S. Bach, chorale, arranged by Jerry Yester. Recording:
    Jerry Yester: Pass Your Light Around; MFQ, Live in Japan.

Publication: *Songs and Sonnets*.

Have a Cigar. 1971. Music: Larry Beckett. Recording: Larry Beckett, private; Jerry Yester, private.

Goethe's Mignon. 1979. Translation of Mignonslied, Johann Goethe. Music: Larry Beckett. Recording: private. Music: 2018, Chris Slusarenko, as The Accidental Falls. Recording: Eyelids, The Accidental Falls.

Across the Persian Gulf. 1978. Music: Christ lag in todesbanden, J. S. Bach, chorale, arranged by Jerry Yester. Recording: Larry Beckett, private; Jerry Yester, Pass Your Light Around; The Association, single, Just The Right Sound: The Association Anthology. Publication: *Songs and Sonnets*.

Love Is on the Street. 1971. Music: Larry Beckett. Recording: private.

Across the Highway. 1973. Music: Jerry Yester. Recording: private.

I Love a Waitress. 1974. Music: Larry Beckett. Recording: private.

Don't You Leave Cheyenne. 1974. Music: Larry Beckett. Recording: private.

My Blue Piano. 1976. Music: Larry Beckett. Recording: private. Publication: *Songs and Sonnets*.

One-Minute Love Affair. 1977. Music: Larry Beckett. Recording: private. Publication: *Songs and Sonnets*.

Sugar Daddy. 1978. Music: Jerry Yester. Recording: Larry Beckett, private; Jerry Yester, Pass Your Light Around; Phoenix 9.

Song to the Air. 1980. Music: Larry Beckett. Recording: private.

Italian Journey. 1983. Music: My Ain Countrie, Scottish song. Recording: private. Publication: *Songs and Sonnets*.

Second Avenue. 1985. Music: Liebster Gott, wann werd' ich sterben, J. S. Bach, chorale, arranged by Jerry Yester. Recording: private. Publication: Ray Gun, Dec.-Jan. 1993; broadside, Rainy Day Women Press; *Songs and Sonnets*.

Old Beauty

All I Can Do Is Dance. 1976. Music: Jerry Yester. Recording: Pass Your Light Around. Publication: *Songs and Sonnets*.

Starlight. 1971. Music: Larry Beckett. Recording: private. Music:

2015, Matt Appleton. Recording: One More Mile. Music: 2018,
    Chris Slusarenko. Recording: Eyelids, The Accidental Falls.
Old Beauty. 1976. Music: Larry Beckett. Recording: private.
On the Hook. 1975. Last song sent to Tim Buckley. Music: 2015,
    Stuart Anthony. Recording: One More Mile.
Elvis Presley. 1978. Music: Larry Beckett. Recording: private.
John Lennon. 1986. Music: Larry Beckett. Recording: private.
    Music: 2015, Stuart Anthony. Recording: One More Mile.
Jeff Buckley. 2006. Music: Jerry Yester. Recording: Yester.
After the Last. 2013. Music: Jann Klose. Recording: In Tandem.
Synchronicity. 2015. Music: Stuart Anthony. Recording: One More
    Mile. Music: 2016, Laura Fletcher. Recording: The Long Lost
    Band, single.

Blue Night

Origin. 2009. Allusions to "A Vindication of the False Basilides",
    Jorge Luis Borges.
We Want a Touchdown. 1973. Music: Larry Beckett. Recording:
    private.
Found at the Scene of a Rendezvous that Failed. 1966. Music: Tim
    Buckley. Recording: Larry Beckett, Tim Buckley reissue; The
    Accidental Falls Demos; Eyelids, The Accidental Falls.
Apollinaire's Gypsy. 2020. Translation of La Tzigane, Guillaume
    Apollinaire. Music: Stuart Anthony, as The Gypsy. Recording:
    Mirabeau Bridge.
Dance for Me, Anna Lee. 1974. Music: Jerry Yester. Recording: Jerry
    Yester, Pass Your Light Around; Larry Beckett, private.
The Brooklyn Girl. 1974. Music: Jerry Yester. Recording: MFQ,
    Moonlight Serenade; Jerry Yester, Just Like the Big Time; Pass
    Your Light Around.
Marlene's Lullaby. 1976. Music: Larry Beckett. Recording: private.
The Whiskey Moon. 1974. Music: Larry Beckett. Recording: Larry
    Beckett, private; Jerry Yester, Pass Your Light Around.
The Rose. 1977. Music: Jerry Yester. Recording: Pass Your Light
    Around.
Blue Night. 1981. Music: Larry Beckett. Recording: private.

Bad Girl. 1982. Music: Larry Beckett. Recording: private.

Love's Outlaws. 1982. Music: Larry Beckett. Recording: private.

Dreamboat. 1982. Music: Larry Beckett. Recording: private. Music: 2015, Stuart Anthony. Recording: One More Mile.

Venice. 1982. Music: Johnny My Man, Scottish song. Recording: Larry Beckett, private.

Bad Faith. 1983. Music: Larry Beckett. Recording: private. Music: 2015, Stuart Anthony. Recording: One More Mile.

The Holy Sacramento. 1983. Music: Prehfrakna Ptichka, The Bird Has Come, Bulgarian song, arranged by Jerry Yester. Recording: Just Like the Big Time.

Winter Blues. 1983. Music: Larry Beckett. Recording: Larry Beckett, private; One More Mile. Music: Jerry Yester. Recording: Lovin' Spoonful Spring Demo.

True Words. 1984. Puerto Penasco, Sonora, Mexico. Music: Larry Beckett. Recording: private.

Boston. 1990. Music: Jerry Yester. Recording: private.

Dante's Answer. 1993. Translation of Io sono stato con Amore insieme, Dante Alighieri.

Mermaid Blues. 2005. Music: Larry Beckett. Recording: private. Music: Jerry Yester. Recording: Yester. Music: 2018, John Moen. Recording: Eyelids, The Accidental Falls.

Thorn & Rose. 2012. Music: Diana Rosalind Trimble, Rudiger Oppermann and Ben-tai Trawinski. Recording: Klang Welten.

River. 2013. Music: Diana Rosalind Trimble. Recording: private. Music: 2018, Chris Slusarenko. Recording: Eyelids, The Accidental Falls.

Flux. 2016. Translation from *Erotocritos*, Vitzentzos Kornaros. Music: Stuart Anthony. Recording: Love & Trial.

Exile and the Kingdom. 2018. Translation from *Erotocritos*, Vitzentzos Kornaros, and "Exile and the Kingdom", Albert Camus. Music: Stuart Anthony. Recording: Love & Trial.

Wild Rose. 2018. Translation from *Erotocritos*, Vitzentzos Kornaros. Music: Stuart Anthony. Recording: Love & Trial.

Insomnia. 2018. Music: John Moen. Recording: Eyelids, The Accidental Falls.

Dream. 2018. Music: John Moen. Recording: Eyelids,

The Accidental Falls.

At Sea. 2018. Music: Chris Slusarenko. Recording: Eyelids,
The Accidental Falls.

Noah's Dove. For Laura Mason Fletcher.

Noah's Dove. 1981. Music: Larry Beckett. Recording: private.

Outlaw Moon. 1981. Music: Larry Beckett. Recording: private.

Talking Gypsy. 1985. Allusions to The Gypsy Laddie, American
version. Music: Larry Beckett. Recording: private.

The Twenty-Sixth of June. 1987. Music: Larry Beckett. Recording:
private.

Ceremony. 1998. Music: 2018, John Moen. Recording: Eyelids,
The Accidental Falls.

Passion. 1988. Music: Larry Beckett. Recording: private. Music:
2018, John Moen. Recording: Eyelids, The Accidental Falls.

Lullaby. 1989. Music: Larry Beckett. Recording: private.

Oh Susannah. 1994. Music: Oats, Peas, Beans, and Barley,
American song. Recording: private.

Liam's Eyes. 2000. Music: Adapted from There Was a Lady, Scottish
song. Recording: private.

To Leda. 2011. Allusions to *A Vision*, 1925 version, W. B. Yeats.

Paradise. 2019. Music: Times a-Getting Hard, American song.
Recording: private.

To Kieran. 2023. Music: Larry Beckett. Recording: private.

Music.

1991. Song cycle. Allusions to *The White Goddess*, Robert Graves.
Music: Wolfgang Mozart, arranged by Jerry Yester. Recording:
MFQ, Wolfgang.

1, 2, 3. Music: String Quintet 6, Mvt. 2, K. 614. Music: 2018, Chris
Slusarenko. Recording: Eyelids, The Accidental Falls.

What Was It. Music: String Quintet 4, Mvt. 1, K. 516.

If It's Magic: Music: Adagio, K. 356.

In the Back. 2002.

Oh the Story. Music: Piano Concerto 21, Mvt. 2, K. 467.

How Do I. 2003. Music: Jerry Yester. Recording: Phoenix 9.
Love in Return. Music: Vesperae solennes, Laudate Dominum,
    K. 339.
I Don't Know. Music: Piano Sonata 11, Mvt. 1, K. 331.
I Have Loved. Music: Eine Kleine Nachtmusik, Mvt. 2, K. 525

The Song. 2017. Music: Stuart Anthony. Recording: Love & Trial.

Acknowledgments

Second Avenue
appeared in Ray Gun, Dec.-Jan. 1993.

All I Can Do Is Dance
Love Lie Down
The Sun Is Like a Big Brass Band
My Blue Piano
Across the Persian Gulf
One-Minute Love Affair
Italian Journey
Second Avenue
appeared in *Songs and Sonnets*, Rainy Day Women Press, 2002.

Canzone alla sirena
with Roberto Cipolat.

Song to the Siren

> Long afloat on shipless oceans,
> I did all my best to smile
> till your singing eyes and fingers
> drew me loving to your isle.

I was in love in 1967, and the love was going nowhere. She was a beauty, she teased me on, and I don't know what was in her heart: but I knew it would have been easier to look into the sun than talk to her about my longing.

> And you sang, Sail to me, sail to me,
> let me enfold you:
> here I am, here I am,
> waiting to hold you.

I wrote lyrics to her; I extended a metaphor, in old ballad form, in trochaic tetrameter, using Homer's imagery. It was just like me in those days: I divided myself into mind and heart, I believed in my mind, and while I was scared of my heart, I was fascinated by it. I wrote my songs using my mind, but out of that fascination.

> Did I dream you dreamt about me?
> Were you hare when I was fox?
> Now my foolish boat is leaning
> broken, lovelorn, on your rocks.

The next morning I took it to the singer at his breakfast, and he looked at it too briefly to read it, and just laid it out of the way, like uninteresting mail. When his breakfast was over, he reached back for his big guitar, like always, and started doodling. Surprisingly, he shoved my page of words back in front of him.

> For you sing, Touch me not, touch me not,
> come back tomorrow.
> Oh my heart, oh my heart
> shies from the sorrow.

It was like a miracle. He sang it out as though it were an old song: he was composing, but the changes he made were little, as though he were only fitting the song to himself. There were two or three other friends at the round table, but not moving it was so moving: we were all listening to that dragging, grieving melody for the first time.

> I am puzzled as the oyster,
> I am troubled as the tide:
> should I stand amid the breakers?
> Should I lie with death my bride?

My lyrics had come alive, like those oriental paper flowers, all folded flat, which, when you drop them into a bowl of water, blossom, and his melody had found an occasion to float out of possibility, into the common air. He and I always loved this song above all others we wrote; the music had a passion that was beyond my daring, the words had a clarity that was beyond his discipline: it was like a handshake of fire between one too thoughtful and one too thoughtless.

> Hear me sing, Swim to me, swim to me,
> let me enfold you:
> here I am, here I am,
> waiting to hold you.

We worked together for a few years, the singer and I, symbols to each other of passion and reason: in the face of each other, we couldn't be complacent, be ourselves—we instinctively knew what Goethe taught, "Take into yourself that which is opposed to you," echoing the ambiguous Greek Heraclitus, who centuries before said, "It is the opposite which is good for us." We grew towards each other, our polarities kept us apart: but across the distance we stretched a song.

Chanson à la sirène

Longtemps sur des océans sans navire,
je faisais de mon mieux pour sourire
avant que tes yeux chantants et tes doigts
m'attirent amoureux vers ton île.

Et tu as chanté, Vogue vers moi, vogue vers moi,
laisse-moi t'enlacer:
je suis là, je suis là,
attendant de t'embrasser.

Ai-je rêvé que tu rêvais de moi?
Étais-tu lièvre quand j'étais renard?
Maintenant mon bête bateau se penche
brisé, délaissé, sur tes rochers.

Car tu chantes, Ne me touche pas, ne me touche pas,
reviens demain.
Oh mon coeur, oh mon coeur
se dérobe au chagrin.

Je suis aussi mystifié que l'huitre,
je suis aussi troublé que la marée:
devrais-je me tenir parmi les brisants?
où m'allonger avec la mort, ma mariée?

Écoute-moi chanter, Nage vers moi, nage vers moi,
laisse-moi t'enlacer:
je suis là, je suis là,
attendant de t'embrasser.

Canzone alla sirena

A lungo su oceani senza navi,
ho fatto di tutto per sorridere,
finché i tuoi occhi, cantando, e le tue dita
m'hanno attratto, amorevole, alla tua isola.

E cantavi, Naviga verso me, naviga verso me,
fatti abbracciare:
eccomi, eccomi
aspetto di stringerti.

Ho sognato che mi sognavi?
Eri lepre quando ero volpe?
Ora la mia sciocca barca pende,
spezzata, affranta, sulle tue rocce.

Perché canti, Non toccarmi, non toccarmi,
torna domani.
Oh il mio cuore, oh il mio cuore
rifugge dal dolore.

Sono perplesso come l'ostrica,
sono turbolento come la marea::
dovrei restare tra le onde?
Dovrei giacere con la morte, mia sposa?

Ascoltami cantare, Nuota verso me, nuota verso me,
fatti abbracciare:
eccomi, eccomi
aspetto di stringerti.

Music is a song cycle. The word "music" is from muse, the goddess who inspires, as in the nine muses of Greek mythology, a survival from prehistory, when god was a woman. Other versions of her include the three Greek fates, Roman moon goddesses, Scandinavian weird sisters, Macbeth's witches. She comes in three forms: bride, woman, hag; and has two competing for her love: bright man, dark rival. The whole story is best told in the *Mabinogion*, a collection of Celtic myths, and *The White Goddess*, a study of them by Robert Graves. It is the story of the changing seasons, and the song cycle is about that, and going out of inspiration and into it, out of love and into it.

	Theme	Song	Mabinogion	Season	Phase
1	Introduction: Calendar	1, 2, 3		Year: Nov — Oct	
2	Solitude	What Was It		Fall	
3	Hag	If It's Magic	Cerridwen	Winter	Old moon
4	Dark rival	In the Back	Gronw	July — Dec	
5	Bride	Oh the Story	Blodeuwedd	Spring	New moon
6	Bright Man	How Do I	Llew	Jan — June	
7	Woman	Love in Return	Rhiannon	Summer	Full moon
8	Company	I Don't Know		Summer	
9	Conclusion: Summary	I Have Loved		Year: Nov — Oct	